The INSIDE GUIDE

FAMOUS NATIVE AMERICANS

Black Elk

By Sophie Washburne

I0807200

Cavendish Square

Published in 2025 by Cavendish Square Publishing, LLC
2544 Clinton Street Buffalo, NY 14224

Copyright © 2025 by Cavendish Square Publishing, LLC

First Edition

No part of this publication may be reproduced, stored in a retrieval system, or transmitted in any form or by any means—electronic, mechanical, photocopying, recording, or otherwise—without the prior permission of the copyright owner. Request for permission should be addressed to Permissions, Cavendish Square Publishing, 2544 Clinton Street Buffalo, NY 14224. Tel (877) 980-4450; fax (877) 980-4454.

Website: cavendishsq.com

This publication represents the opinions and views of the author based on their personal experience, knowledge, and research. The information in this book serves as a general guide only. The author and publisher have used their best efforts in preparing this book and disclaim liability rising directly or indirectly from the use and application of this book.

All websites were available and accurate when this book was sent to press.

Library of Congress Cataloging-in-Publication Data

Names: Washburne, Sophie, author.
Title: Black Elk / Sophie Washburne.
Description: Buffalo, NY : Cavendish Square Publishing, [2025] | Series: The inside guide : famous Native Americans | Includes bibliographical references and index.
Identifiers: LCCN 2023059220 | ISBN 9781502671042 (library binding) | ISBN 9781502671035 (paperback) | ISBN 9781502671059 (ebook)
Subjects: LCSH: Black Elk, 1863-1950–Juvenile literature. | Oglala Indians–Biography–Juvenile literature. | Oglala Indians–Religion–Juvenile literature.
Classification: LCC E99.O3 B5397 2025 | DDC 978.004/9752440092 a B–dc23/eng/20240214
LC record available at https://lccn.loc.gov/2023059220

Editor: Jennifer Lombardo
Copyeditor: Jill Keppeler
Designer: Deanna Lepovich

The photographs in this book are used by permission and through the courtesy of: Cover Everett Collection Inc/Alamy Stock Photo; p. 4 Zack Frank/Shutterstock.com; p. 6 neftali/Shutterstock.com; pp. 7, 16, 28 (left) Everett Collection/Shutterstock.com; p. 9 Danita Delimont/Alamy Stock Photo; p. 10 Don Mammoser/Shutterstock.com; p. 12 Iryna Marienko/Shutterstock.com; p. 13 Aaron J Hill/Shutterstock.com; p. 14 Photo Spirit/Shutterstock.com; pp. 18, 28 (right), 29 (left) courtesy of the Library of Congress; p. 19 Black Elk and Elk of the Oglala Lakota -1887/Wikimedia Commons; p. 21 Gerwin Schadl/Shutterstock.com; p. 22 Pierre Jean Durieu/Shutterstock.com; p. 24 Stephen Saks Photography/Alamy Stock Photo; p. 26 Tami Freed/Shutterstock.com; p. 29 (right) lynea/Shutterstock.com.

Some of the images in this book illustrate individuals who are models. The depictions do not imply actual situations or events.

CPSIA compliance information: Batch #CSCSQ25: For further information contact Cavendish Square Publishing LLC at 1-877-980-4450.

Printed in the United States of America

Find us on

CONTENTS

Black Elk's tribe lived in the Black Hills of South Dakota and Wyoming.

Chapter One

CHILDHOOD VISIONS

Black Elk was likely born in December 1863, near the Little Powder River in what is now the state of Wyoming. He was the fourth man in his family to be named Black Elk. His father, grandfather, and great-grandfather were all also given that name. Black Elk and his family belonged to the Oglala Lakota—one of the groups that make up the Great Sioux Nation.

Early Life

Today, people often think of childhood as being a time of fun and happiness. Kids play with their friends, go to school, and enjoy time with their family. However, when Black Elk was a child, his people were in danger from the white **colonizers** who had come to what is now the United States.

> **Fast Fact**
>
> Although they have adopted the name "Sioux," people who are part of this nation prefer to be called by whichever band they belong to.

From a very young age, Black Elk knew the adults in his life were worried about white people coming to kill their tribe and take their

TRIBES OF THE GREAT SIOUX NATION

Dakota	Nakota	Lakota
Waqpekute	Yankton	Teton
Wahepton	Yanktonais	Subtribes of the Teton:
Sisseton		Oglala
Mdewankantonwan		Brule
		Two Kettle
		Sans Arc
		Blackfeet
		Hunkpapa
		Minneconjou

Shown here is one way people have grouped the Sioux peoples. However, the Yankton and Yanktonais are sometimes considered Dakota groups.

Crazy Horse was a chief and warrior of the Oglala Lakota. Black Elk admired him very much.

Fast Fact

When Black Elk was a child, battle was an important part of the Sioux culture, or way of life. Many children's games involved fighting as practice for becoming honored and respected warriors when they were older.

lands. His father was wounded in a battle with white men when Black Elk was three years old. The Oglala also fought with other Native American groups. However, daily life went on. Black Elk's grandfather gave him his first bow and arrow, and Black Elk used it to hunt small animals such as frogs and squirrels. Black Elk also went fishing and played games with his friends. One game involved **wrestling** on horseback until one person was thrown to the ground.

The Spanish brought horses to what is now the United States. By 1680, horses had become an important part of the Lakota culture.

BLACK ELK SPEAKS

In 1932, an author named John Neihardt published a book called *Black Elk Speaks*. Neihardt interviewed Black Elk about his life and wrote down what he said. The book became very popular—and very **controversial**. Neihardt was not Native American, and many Sioux say he didn't do a very good job explaining their culture.

Even though the book is written as if in Black Elk's own words, there are some places where Neihardt left things out or added things he thought would sound good. The basic information in the book came from Black Elk, but readers should know that not everything written in the book was actually spoken by him.

The Great Vision

Black Elk had visions throughout his life, starting when he was around four years old. At first, he heard voices calling his name when there were no other people around. Later, he saw things as well. When he was five, he had a vision of two men coming out of the clouds and singing, "A sacred voice is calling you." He did not tell anyone about this vision because it scared him.

When he was eight or nine years old, Black Elk got very sick. While he was sick, he had another vision. This one started with the same men he had seen when he was five. He said they led him to a place in the sky, where he met a group called the Six Grandfathers. These six men represented north, south, east, west, Earth, and the sky. They showed

One of the gifts the Six Grandfathers gave Black Elk was a peace pipe similar to this one. This gift meant Black Elk would be a great healer when he was older.

Black Elk what would happen to the Lakota and other Native Americans in the years to come. Black Elk also said the Six Grandfathers gave him gifts that were meant to give him power so he could help his people.

Fast Fact

When Black Elk woke from his vision, his parents told him he had been asleep for 12 days. He kept his vision a secret for several years because he was afraid no one would believe that a child had seen such important things.

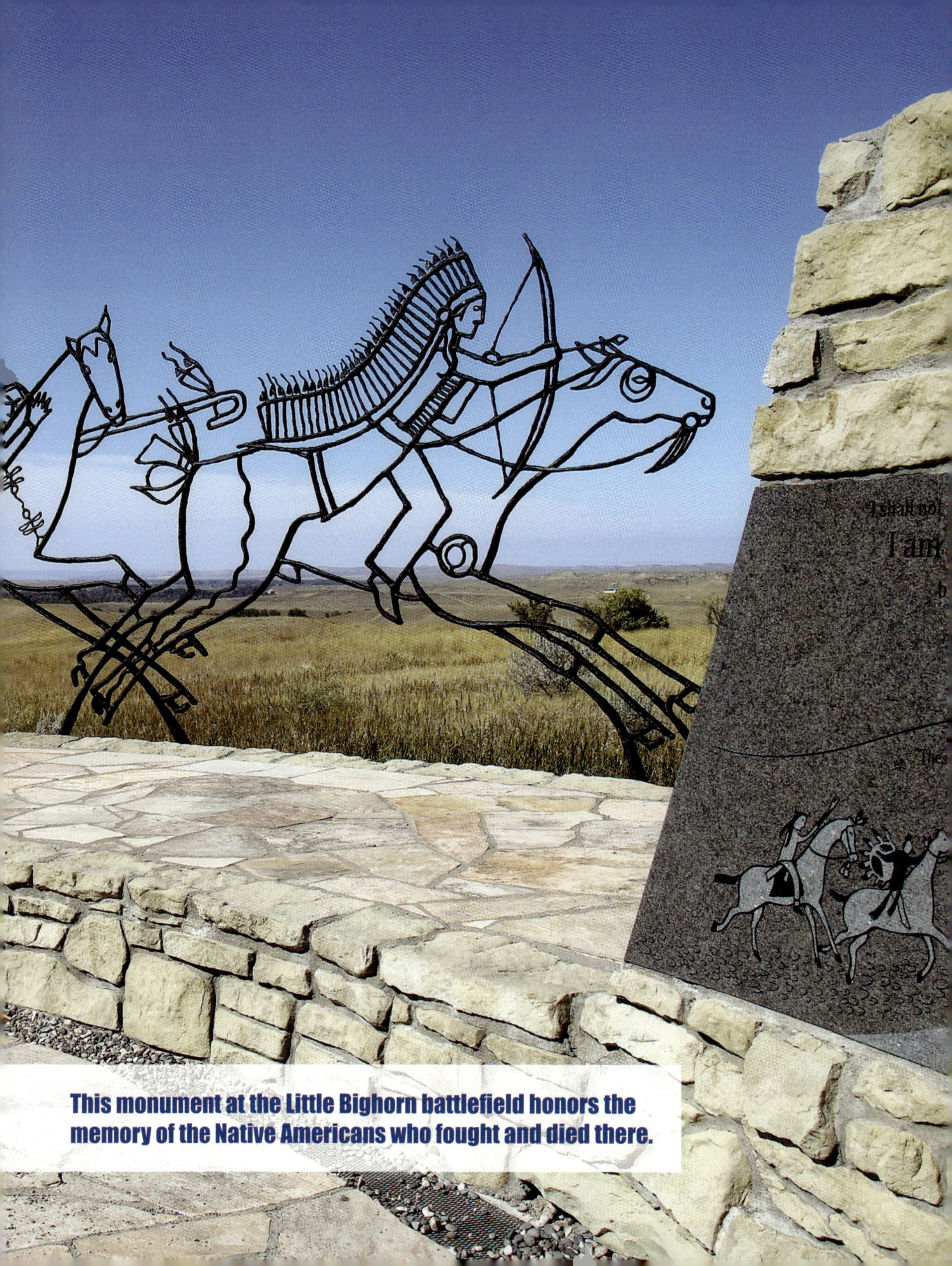

This monument at the Little Bighorn battlefield honors the memory of the Native Americans who fought and died there.

A BATTLE AND A DANCE

Chapter Two

The Battle of the Little Bighorn is a well-known battle in American history. On one side were the Lakota warriors. On the other were American soldiers, led by Lieutenant Colonel George Custer, or "Long Hair," as the Lakota called him. The battle was named by white Americans after the place where it was fought—near the Little Bighorn River, in what is now the state of Montana. The Lakota call it the Battle of the Greasy Grass.

Black Elk on the Battlefield

Black Elk was about 12 years old when the U.S. Army arrived in Lakota territory to force the Native Americans out of the Black Hills. The battle began a little after noon on June 25, 1876. Custer thought the battle would be easily won, but he soon realized that the Lakota and their allies, or friends—the Dakota, Cheyenne, and Arapaho—were better fighters than he had expected. Custer was killed at the Battle of the Little Bighorn, which gave the battle another nickname: Custer's Last Stand.

Fast Fact

Today, the Little Bighorn battlefield is part of a national monument. People can visit it and see where the battle took place.

MAKING AND BREAKING A TREATY

For many years, the Lakota fought against the white colonizers who wanted to take their land. In 1868, some Lakota leaders agreed to sign a treaty with the American government. This treaty, called the Treaty of Fort Laramie, created a reservation, or land set aside just for the Lakota. Part of the reservation included the Black Hills of South Dakota and Wyoming.

In 1874, the army ordered George Custer to explore the Black Hills, even though this **violated** the treaty. When the group that Custer was leading found gold there, the U.S. government tried to buy the land from the Lakota. They refused to sell, but the government ordered them to move by January 31, 1876. When the Lakota ignored this order, the government sent troops to force the Lakota to move anyway.

The Black Hills have been sacred to the Lakota for hundreds of years. As of 2024, they are still fighting to have ownership of the land returned to them.

Black Elk was too young to take part in most of the battle. However, he was allowed on the battlefield to take clothing and weapons from dead and dying soldiers. He later said that he was proud and happy that he had helped his people defend themselves.

These markers on the Little Bighorn battlefield are memorials for the American soldiers who died in the battle.

The Horse Dance

When Black Elk was about 16, he said, he started to feel very scared nearly all the time, especially when he heard thunder. It reminded him of his vision, especially the two men who had come out of the clouds to speak to him. He would often hear voices that seemed

Fast Fact

Black Elk's fear may have been caused by post-traumatic stress disorder (PTSD), although there was no word for it at the time. His visions had scared him very badly when he was young.

Black Elk spent time in a sweat lodge, such as the one shown here, to make himself pure before performing the horse dance to help his fear go away. This is still part of some Native American traditions today.

to be coming from the animals around him. The voices would say things such as, "It is time!"

Black Elk was scared that he would have another vision. His fear was so strong that he began to have a hard time sleeping, getting along with people, and doing everyday things. His parents were so worried about him that they brought him to see a medicine man named Black Road. Black Elk was tired of being scared, so he told Black Road all about his vision.

Fast Fact

After the horse dance, Black Elk said that many Lakota who had been sick came to tell him that they were healthy again. This was how the tribe knew Black Elk was meant to be a medicine man.

Black Road said that Black Elk would stop being afraid if he shared his vision with the rest of the tribe. Black Road told Black Elk to perform a **ceremony** called the horse dance. After the ceremony, Black Elk's fear went away, and he was recognized as a medicine man by his tribe.

Buffalo Bill Cody (*right*) is shown here with Sitting Bull (*left*). Buffalo Bill's traveling show created many of the ideas we still have today about what the "Wild West" was like.

BUFFALO BILL AND WOUNDED KNEE

Chapter Three

In 1886, a group of white men came to the Oglala Lakota and asked if any of them would like to join a traveling show. The show, which was run by William "Buffalo Bill" Cody, showed people in cities a **romanticized** idea of what the Western part of what is now the United States was like. Black Elk agreed to join the show because he wanted to learn more about white people's culture. He wanted to bring any good ideas they had back to his people to help make their lives better.

Traveling with Buffalo Bill

Buffalo Bill's show went to cities around the world. Performers would do tricks on horseback, show off their shooting skills, and stage pretend battles between the white and Native American performers.

Behind the scenes, the Native Americans were generally treated the same as the other performers. They were also **encouraged** to keep practicing their culture and

> **Fast Fact**
>
> The show Black Elk joined, which was called Buffalo Bill's Wild West, toured from 1884 to 1915. Black Elk was part of the show for three years, from the ages of 22 to 25.

This poster for Buffalo Bill's Wild West shows Native Americans fighting with Americans who were moving West in a wagon train. This kind of fight was often shown in Western shows and movies, but it hardly ever happened in real life.

language. However, in the show, the Native Americans were presented as wild **savages**. They wore costumes they would not often wear in real life, and in fake battles, they were often

Fast Fact

On the day Buffalo Bill's Wild West started to travel back to the United States from England, Black Elk and several other Lakota performers got lost on the way to the boat and were left behind. They joined a different Wild West show until Buffalo Bill's show returned to Europe.

A WEST THAT NEVER WAS

Buffalo Bill's Wild West was a very successful show. Audiences around the world loved the staged fights and gunplay. White men especially liked it because it showed white people as brave and powerful fighters who tamed a wild enemy—the Native Americans.

Buffalo Bill presented the show as historical fact even though he had made most of it up for entertainment, so many people who saw it came to believe this was how the West truly was. Because travel was hard and expensive in those days, few people would ever see the West for themselves. Movies and TV shows called Westerns later made this kind of entertainment available to an even wider audience. These myths, or stories, about the Wild West are still repeated today.

This picture of Black Elk (*left*) was taken while he was traveling with Buffalo Bill's Wild West.

shown as bloodthirsty so audiences would cheer when they lost. Such performances made it hard for white audiences to see Native Americans as real people with their own cultures.

Buffalo Bill's show took Black Elk to places such as New York City and London, England. He did not like what he saw of white culture. After a short time, Black Elk became homesick. He returned to the Lakota reservation in 1889.

Wounded Knee

When Black Elk returned home, he found that the Lakota reservation was half the size it had been when he left. The U.S. government had violated the treaty again and taken more of the land. The Lakota were starving and sick. They were angry that the government kept breaking its promises.

In times of trouble, people often turn to a god or gods for help. This was what the Lakota did. A Paiute man named Wovoka had started a religion, or faith, that combined Native American and Christian ideas. It was known as the Ghost Dance.

The U.S. government was worried about the growing popularity of Wovoka and the Ghost Dance. In 1890, about 500 U.S. soldiers arrived at Wounded Knee Creek, where the Ghost Dance ceremonies were often performed. They started shooting the mostly

Fast Fact

The U.S. government wanted to make Native Americans act exactly like white people. For this reason, a law called the Religious Crimes Code of 1883 made it illegal for Native Americans to practice their religious ceremonies, such as the Ghost Dance.

unarmed Lakota. Black Elk was nearby and went to help his people when he heard the guns. He and other Lakota men fought back against the soldiers and worked to move some of the Lakota to a safe place.

Today, a monument stands on a mass Lakota grave at the site of the Wounded Knee Massacre. Between 150 and 300 Lakota were killed there by American soldiers.

Today, Native Americans of all tribes can often openly celebrate their culture. This picture was taken in 2018 at the 49th annual United Tribes International Powwow.

LATER LIFE

Chapter Four

Wounded Knee marked a turning point for Native Americans in the United States—not just the Lakota but all tribes across the country. The horror of the event made them largely unwilling to continue fighting openly against white Americans. They did not want to see more of their people murdered.

Religious Conversion

Two years after Wounded Knee, Black Elk married a woman named Katie War Bonnet. They had three boys together. The family lived on the Pine Ridge reservation, where Black Elk fulfilled his childhood vision by becoming a medicine man.

> **Fast Fact**
>
> Although there were no more major battles between the U.S. Army and Native Americans after Wounded Knee, Native Americans did not completely give up their resistance. They practiced parts of their culture in secret and staged peaceful protests.

Black Elk's oldest son died around 1895, and Katie War Bonnet died a few years later. Of course, these two events made Black Elk very

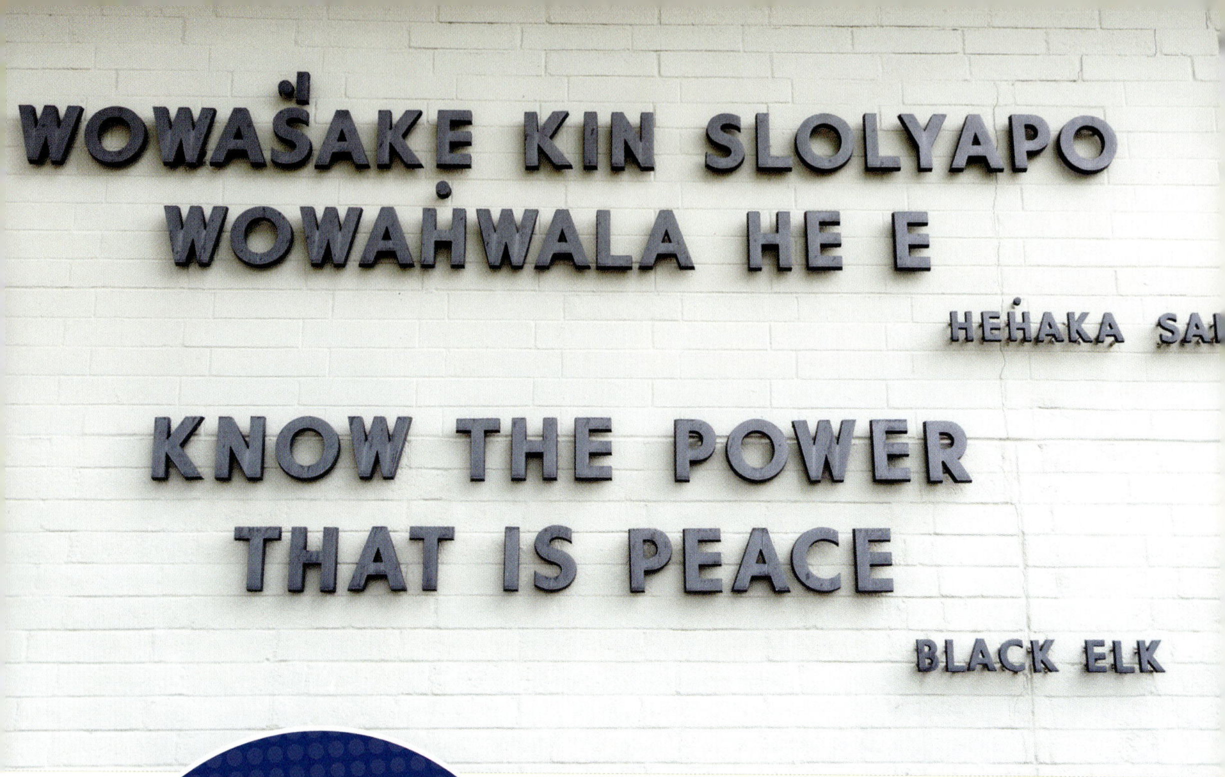

This quote by Black Elk is written in both Lakota and English.

Fast Fact

Black Elk converted to Christianity because he wanted to. However, many Native Americans were forced to convert, and their traditional religions were outlawed by the government.

sad. He wanted to find a way to feel peaceful again. Many other Lakota had converted, or changed their religion, to a kind of Christianity called Catholicism. Black Elk began to think about converting as well. He did so in 1904, when he was almost 40 years old. As part of his conversion, he took on a new Christian name. He became known as Nicholas Black Elk.

BLACK ELK'S CONVERSION STORY

Black Elk remarried in 1906 and had more children, including a daughter named Lucy. He told the story of his conversion to Lucy, and she told it to others after Black Elk died.

In 1904, Black Elk went to the home of a young boy who was very sick. He was there as a medicine man to try to heal the boy. While he was there, a priest arrived at the boy's home. He threw away all the medicine Black Elk had made and prayed over the boy instead. When the priest saw that Black Elk was upset, he offered Black Elk a ride to the mission, or building where he lived with other priests.

At the mission, Black Elk was given new clothes, a meal, and a place to sleep for the night. Black Elk felt that God had sent the priest to him to show him a new way of living. He converted to Catholicism two weeks after he arrived at the mission.

Fast Fact

When he was an adult, Black Elk had an accident that partially blinded him. The exact details of the accident are unknown, but what is certain is that it involved gunpowder exploding in Black Elk's face.

Spreading Christianity

After he converted, Black Elk was no longer a medicine man in the Lakota tradition, or way, but he was still respected by the Lakota as a religious leader. Instead of healing the sick, he spent the rest of his life

In Black Elk's major childhood vision, he was standing on what is now known as Black Elk Peak.

spreading Christianity and helping the Lakota. He blended some of the Lakota traditions with his Catholic faith. For example, he still smoked the sacred pipe that was part of the Lakota religious tradition. This blend of faiths helped him bridge the gap between the Lakota and white Christian Americans, making him an effective leader.

Black Elk died in 1950 around the age of 84. He is remembered by Native Americans and white Americans alike as a holy man and great leader. In 2016, the U.S. government renamed South Dakota's highest mountain after Black Elk. For many years, the mountain had been known as Harney Peak, after General William S. Harney. Many Lakota found it offensive that one of their sacred peaks was named after a man who had taken part in a Lakota massacre in 1855. They felt that renaming it was a good way to honor Black Elk.

In 2017, the Catholic Church began the process of canonizing Black Elk, or making him a saint. Through these memorials, Black Elk again bridged a gap. He was honored the Lakota way, through nature, and the white Christian way, through sainthood.

THINK ABOUT IT!

1. How do you think Black Elk was affected by growing up in a time when his loved ones were in danger of being killed?
2. Why do you think Black Elk was so scared of his visions?
3. What problems were caused by presenting Buffalo Bill's Wild West as historical fact?
4. Why do you think Black Elk converted to Christianity?

TIMELINE

Black Elk's Life	World Events
1863 Black Elk is born.	**1863** President Abraham Lincoln issues the Emancipation Proclamation.
early 1870s Black Elk has an important vision.	
1876 Black Elk is present at the Battle of the Little Bighorn.	**1877** Thomas Edison invents the phonograph.
	1883 Krakatoa volcano creates largest explosion in modern history.
	1885 Louis Pasteur creates the first successful rabies vaccine.
1886–1889 Black Elk tours with Buffalo Bill.	
1890 Black Elk fights at Wounded Knee Massacre.	
1892 Black Elk marries Katie War Bonnet.	**1892** The *Nutcracker* ballet premieres.
	1896 First modern Olympics are held.
	1939 World War II begins.
1950 Black Elk dies.	

GLOSSARY

ceremony: A formal act or series of acts performed in some regular way according to fixed rules.

colonizer: A person who moves to another country to live on land that was taken from a Native group.

controversial: Causing an expression of opposing views.

encourage: To cause to feel courage or hope.

massacre: The violent and cruel killing of a group of people.

post-traumatic stress disorder: A mental illness that happens to someone after they go through a very upsetting event, characterized by anxiety, flashbacks, and avoidance of things that remind them of the event.

romanticize: To treat as idealized or heroic.

savage: A person who is brutal and uncivilized.

violate: To fail to keep or observe.

wrestling: A sport in which two opponents try to unbalance each other.

FIND OUT MORE

Books

Doyle, Abby Badach. *Black Elk*. New York, NY: Enslow Publishing, 2023.

Nelson, S. D. *Crazy Horse and Custer: Born Enemies*. New York, NY: Abrams Books for Young Readers, 2021.

Treuer, David, and Sheila Keenan. *The Heartbeat of Wounded Knee: Life in Native America*. New York, NY: Viking, 2022.

Websites

Ducksters: Wounded Knee Massacre
www.ducksters.com/history/native_americans/wounded_knee_massacre.php
Read about what happened at Wounded Knee in 1890.

Kiddle: Black Elk Facts for Kids
kids.kiddle.co/Black_Elk
Learn more about Black Elk's life.

National Parks Service: The Lakota Emergence Story
www.nps.gov/wica/learn/historyculture/the-lakota-emergence-story.htm
Read or listen to a Lakota myth about where the tribe came from.

Publisher's note to educators and parents: Our editors have carefully reviewed these websites to ensure that they are suitable for students. Many websites change frequently, however, and we cannot guarantee that a site's future contents will continue to meet our high standards of quality and educational value. Be advised that students should be closely supervised whenever they access the internet.

INDEX